Unexpected Hope

Ridhima Batra

Published by "The Great Indian Book Tour"

Imprint : **Holistic Publishing**

www.tgibt.com

Phone : +91-72400-68114

email : prashant@tgibt.com

Title : **Unexpected Hope**

Author : **Ridhima Batra**

First published in 2024

First Edition 2024

ISBN : 978-93-93262-91-2

Price : USD 5

"In the heart of darkness, hope becomes a guiding light, leading lost souls back to themselves. When all seems lost, hope whispers, 'You're not alone', and gently nudges us to find our way amid life's labyrinth. It's the spark that reignites our spirits when we're at our lowest, showing us that even in the shadows, there's a path to rediscover who we are."

What to expect in this book?

"Welcome, dear readers, to a world where enchantment meets reality, where the unexpected unveils itself as hope. Within the chapters of 'Unexpected Hope: The Enchanted Stories', lies a tapestry woven with tales of resilience, transformation, and the magical essence of hope. Each story, a beacon in the darkest of times, holds a treasure trove of whispers from the universe, guiding you through moments of uncertainty and despair.

As you embark on this journey, let these enchanting narratives serve as companions, gently nudging you toward the light. Through the trials and triumphs of the characters, discover the subtle hints and hidden treasures that mirror your own journey. Within these pages, expect to find unexpected twists that mirror the complexities of life, reminding you that amid chaos and despair, hope is an unwavering force.

Embrace these tales not just as stories but as guides to finding hope where it seems lost. Allow the magic of these narratives to unravel the knots of uncertainty, offering solace and wisdom. Remember, dear reader, that within the unexpected lies the most profound hope, waiting to be discovered."

Acknowledgments

I extend my deepest gratitude to the myriad souls who have woven their presence into the tapestry of my life, guiding me through the labyrinth of inspiration and offering their unwavering support in birthing these tales.

To my family, my grandparents Joginderlal Batra and Motia Batra, my parents Raj Batra and Santosh Batra, my brothers Gautam and Sanat Batra whose ceaseless encouragement and understanding have been the bedrock of my creative journey, I offer my heartfelt thanks. Your patience during the countless hours lost in imagination is a testament to your boundless love.

To my friends, whose laughter and shared adventures injected vibrant hues into the narrative of my days, thank you for being both muse and refuge.

To my mentors and guides, your wisdom has been the beacon illuminating the uncharted paths, allowing me to navigate the realms of storytelling with greater clarity and purpose.

And to the readers, for your willingness to embark upon these enchanted narratives, may these tales offer respite, inspiration, and unexpected hope amid life's vicissitudes.

Chapters

Self-Acceptance

A quest to uncover one's true self is a journey of introspection.

Consider this: When asked "who you are," many respond with a name, a title, or descriptions given by others, failing to encapsulate the essence within. It's an exploration of behavior, personality, and unique traits.

Picture this: In childhood, the yearning to play freely, the stubbornness for one's desires, and the camaraderie with friends without judgment—a time of purity and unbridled activity.

Self-discovery begins by retracing these steps, recalling cherished activities and preferred ways of navigating life's early trials. Examining how relationships evolved sheds light on personal growth. Moreover, how one perceives themselves in solitude—whether with pride or self-doubt—offers crucial insight.

Delve deeper, expand your horizon, and acknowledge latent potentials. Mentor yourself by acknowledging positive values—compassion, kindness, and an innate drive to aid others—and ambitions to perpetually serve humanity.

Chart your answers to these inquiries. Unveil your aspirations, talents, and daily habits. Examine why people gravitate toward or repel from you. Notice the compliments received—do they fortify or dictate your essence? Understanding oneself transcends dependence on external validation.

Emotions wield profound influence; acknowledging their sway empowers self-regulation. Errors are inevitable; it's in their aftermath where personal growth materializes. Do they foster acceptance and progress or breed remorse and stagnation?

Close your eyes. Reflect on moments of newfound talents and problem-solving triumphs—the genesis of self-awareness. Every lesson learned unravels a strand of your narrative.

This voyage culminates in a revelation—an intricate tapestry woven with aspirations, traits, and experiences. A mosaic portraying the unique you—a journey to rediscover the authentic self, unraveling the enigma within.

Inner Harmony

Navigating life often introduces us to a persistent loophole: doubting ourselves. We scrutinize our self-belief, internalizing negativity from external sources and underestimating our innate capabilities. The perceptions shaped by parental, societal, and peer treatment often become our self-imposed labels.

In moments of adversity, the veils thin, revealing those who genuinely care amid a sea of pretense. Yet, the enduring quandary persists—the nagging doubt within ourselves.

Reflecting on my own journey, I've witnessed many grappling with discontentment about their appearance, physique, or mannerisms. Questions linger: uncertainty about life's purpose, occasional existential ponderings, and questioning our very creation and its intent.

Congratulations are due if these thoughts assail your mind; they signify a yearning for enlightenment. Doubts aren't deterrents but indicators prompting a shift, signaling a need for evolution beyond the present state.

A lack of self-love often stems from an absence of reciprocated affection, while doubt in abilities roots in an identity crisis. Seeking validation from others merely underscores a struggle in making personal choices.

Are these feelings inherently wrong? No. They're human. To err is human, and learning emerges from these struggles, fostering growth. Embracing oneself, flaws and all, is the journey toward self-love.

The discomfort with physical appearances, skin color—natural attributes, plague many. True love resides in those who embrace our entirety, imperfections included. Resistance to change from external pressures is a testament to self-acceptance.

In life's grand narrative, one ponders: Whom do we truly seek to impress? Society, family, and friends—all hold significance, yet the essence lies in valuing oneself. A good heart and noble deeds make one extraordinary, outshining transient physical attributes.

Trust in oneself forms the cornerstone. When the curtains fall and wounds surface, it's an individual's journey. Striving for self-improvement, not for external affirmation, but for personal growth and contentment, becomes paramount.

In essence, a good human transcends fleeting physicality. Trust, acceptance, and self-love sculpt an individual's narrative, creating a legacy that extends beyond mere appearances or societal accolades.

Be you.

Make your individuality and love your well-being.

In the end,

You are like a sun who is always shining bright.

Self-Love

To the cores that I have in my head and to all those harsh things I have been through, yet, I see myself as someone who has endured challenges and learned to love myself again.

In life's constant quest, the refrain echoes: "I am not enough." But here's the revelation—you are enough! The incessant feeling of inadequacy often stems from the erroneous belief that worth is dictated by external possessions or achievements.

Pause for a moment and ponder: "Does my worth truly hinge on material possessions?" This reflection may evoke a spectrum of emotions. Allow them to unfurl, for they've long fueled the pursuit of worth outside oneself. Embrace these sensations, allowing them to exist without judgment.

Repeat it to yourself: "You are enough." Embrace

the reality that as a human being, you possess intrinsic value, love, and boundless wonder.

Consider the treasures you possess, the fortunate occurrences that often go unnoticed. Cease doubting your abilities; embrace your inherent strength. Recall the moments when the brink of surrender was near, yet resilience prevailed—testament to your latent power.

You transcend the confines of familial ties, friendships, and societal norms. Your life is a tapestry woven with threads of joy and happiness. Embrace it, cherish it, for it is yours—unique and unrepeatable.

Embrace self-love and acceptance; therein lies the key. When you affirm yourself, the universe mirrors that love back to you. Your uniqueness is unparalleled, a masterpiece crafted by life's intricacies.

Contemplate your offerings to the world—your talents, your kindness—and witness how the world reciprocates. Keep giving, keep manifesting, for you are already the best version of yourself.

Remember, amid the chaos and doubts, you are enough. This truth is unwavering. You are enough—allow these words to resonate within you, shaping your journey toward self-acceptance and fulfillment.

Embracing Chaos

Tell me about the last time you read a book, in which you wanted to live forever and you just ended up being sorry for yourself because you couldn't. Tell me about the last time you were awake till 3 am, crying about your lost sweetheart, as if no one but only she loved you. Tell me about the last time you were fucked up and you called every close friend of yours just to curse them for not being with you and ended up making them more close to you. Tell me about the last time you thought of jumping from a running train into a canal, just to calm the chaos in your head. Tell me about the last time you were walking in the rain, drenched completely to get rid of your demons. But you couldn't because they were your demons. Then, tell me there wasn't any last time, that there won't be another time. That you would do all these things over and over again because it's you. That you are the god of small things and you are alive just because of these small things. That there are galaxies within you which can't be figured out, but there will be one who will help you to make something out of them. And you will call the one love.

Self-Discovery

It was a curious exploration into the desires of change that stirred my thoughts. I posed a simple question to acquaintances: "What's the one thing you wish to change about yourself?" To my surprise, the responses resonated with a collective longing for physical alterations. Some yearned to be slender, others for fairness, and some for height, muscle, or even to shed weight.

This prompted me to pose the same question to a young child, expecting a similar desire for physical change. However, her response struck a chord of wonder within me. She expressed contentment, finding comfort and joy in her own skin. Her wish wasn't for physical alterations but for something fantastical—to sprout wings and soar like a bird. Her innocent response left me both amazed and somewhat saddened.

Reflecting on these conversations, it became evident how frequently we seek external validation. How often do we yearn for acceptance, love, and validation from others? The longing to fit into societal molds, to seek approval, and to constantly question how others perceive us—it's a narrative many of us share.

I pondered, when was the last time I—or anyone—uttered affirmations of self-love? How many times have we embraced ourselves wholly, irrespective of societal standards? How many instances have we cherished our own uniqueness?

It's a simple yet profound truth: External forces shouldn't govern our happiness or self-worth. Living to impress oneself, embracing one's authenticity, and steering life's course independent of external judgments is paramount. To love oneself unabashedly, to accept every facet—be it perceived flaws or unique attributes—this is the crux of self-acceptance.

Life's true journey commences with self-love. It's about recognizing that we are enough, we are beautiful, and we are exceptional in our own right. Embracing this truth—loving and accepting ourselves—is where life's true magic begins.

Authenticity Journey

Within me dwell two distinct personas, each emerging under different circumstances. I'm peculiar—I shun the company of many, content in my solitude. I thrive in the tranquility of being alone, away from the hustle and bustle. But amid this self-imposed seclusion, there exists a transformation. For a select few, scarcely one or two, I undergo a metamorphosis—I become affectionate, altruistic, and at times, a tad reliant. It's akin to a switch, toggling between these two personas. Most perceive me as guarded and aloof, strangers encountering my shielded exterior. Yet, for those few privy to my inner world, they'd paint a picture of an innocent, endearing soul.

I relish harboring these contrasting versions within me. One shields me from insincere connections, shielding me from the whims of superficial relationships. The other unveils a realm of genuine human connection, enveloping me in warmth and authenticity. This duality offers me a sanctuary—a castle fortified with trust, love, care, belonging, truth, honesty, and loyalty. Beyond its walls, however, I'm impervious, unwavering against external influences, standing resolute in my strength.

The journey toward this equilibrium demanded copious tears and a mosaic of emotions. I once wept over trifles, deeply affected by the slightest shifts in friendships. I was naively innocent, often heartbroken by the stark contrast between appearances and reality. But with time came resilience—I learned to say no, delineate boundaries, and sever ties that disrupted my peace.

A paramount lesson emerged—to compartmentalize life. I maintain a dichotomy: an inner sanctum graced by a select few and an exterior realm accessible to a broader circle. These worlds don't intermingle. I've learned not to harbor guilt in refusing entry into my inner sanctum. Amid a world teeming with promises, I've discerned the importance of discernment. It's about peering beyond mere words, seeking resonance in souls and energies. Life isn't about encountering the right individuals; it's more about recognizing and sidestepping the wrong ones.

So, embrace your dual lives, cherish the intimate sanctum, and guard it vigilantly. Don't succumb to guilt in setting boundaries. Amid the cacophony of promises, trust the vibrations and energies that ema-

nate from others. For life isn't about welcoming everyone, it's about discerning and sidestepping those who
don't resonate with your essence.

Drifting Wanderers

In the midst of life's challenges, you might feel adrift, uncertain of the path ahead, and torn between self-improvement and settling into a routine that seems comfortable yet lacks fulfillment. It's okay to feel lost, to grapple with the weight of expectations, and to witness others achieving what you aspire to while you're still finding your footing. The pressure to carve a path that brings pride can weigh heavily, leaving you melancholic as you wait for your moment.

But amid this struggle, remember that it's alright to feel that heaviness, that emptiness coursing through your veins. As a human, experiencing these emotions is natural. Yet, within this tumult, find solace in the little things that bring contentment. Embrace the fact that even though you're not precisely where you envision, you're content with the small joys—savoring your favorite morning coffee, learning from past missteps, and diligently working toward your aspirations.

Appreciate the blessings that surround you—a handful of dependable friends, a cozy bed during colder months, the warmth of your parents' prepared meals, the fresh air you breathe, the nostalgic tunes that soothe your soul, and the tenacity in adapting to a new normal while upholding a rigorous study routine. True, you may not embody flawlessness, but recognize that each possession, each moment, is a blessing in its own right. Understand that what you have now is enough; you needn't yearn for more because the blessings meant for you will eventually find their way into your life. Embrace the sufficiency of your existence, knowing that, above all else, you are enough.

Cultivating Inner Balance

There are moments when life feels overwhelming, when you're ensnared in a sense of helplessness. It's a raw and gut-wrenching experience; no comforting words or effort seem to extricate you from that murky quagmire. You might feel trapped, as if you're stuck on a relentless loop. People might dismiss it as a phase, but you'll wonder if there's any respite in sight. Nights blur into sleepless stretches, tears soaking your pillow, days filled with daydreams mingled with self-doubt. Each breath feels heavier, and merely navigating through the day becomes a taxing ordeal. In these bleak moments, ones that corrode hope from within, the hardest but most essential belief to hold onto is in yourself.

I understand how challenging it is to grasp, but it's vital to remind yourself that these phases aren't meant to define your entire life. They're segments—

some longer than others—that you must navigate through. Yet, these trying episodes, these fragmented parts, hold invaluable lessons. They bring you closer to understanding your essence, unveiling aspects about yourself and the world that traditional teachings often overlook. Amid unfamiliar terrains, you discover fragility and kindness, unearthing reservoirs of strength within when you least expect it.

These phases resemble seasons; just when you believe the frosty winters will persist endlessly, you stumble upon March, realizing it was an arduous but transient season. Similarly, when you find yourself indulging in ice cream before bedtime, seeking refuge indoors, you experience October, understanding that everything has its part to play. Nothing is perpetual, and just like the seasons, these phases too shall pass.

It's crucial to view these fragments of life as transient seasons—each holding its own purpose. The key is embracing the belief that these phases will eventually fade, and until then, your resilience will help you weather through. Life is a tapestry woven with both the good and the bad, often blurring the distinction between the two. And as long as you persevere, discovering yourself and believing in your resilience even amid hopelessness, that's what truly defines living—for each and every one of us.

Sincere Vulnerability

Anxiety, a pervasive struggle faced by many, often feels like an incessant weight pressing down upon us, relentless in its presence. We try to mask it, bury it deep, but it invariably resurfaces, creeping back into our consciousness. The truth is, external factors frequently sow the seeds of this unease. It could stem from the relentless pressure to excel, conform, or achieve an unattainable perfection. Perhaps it's the fear of the unknown, the future's uncertainties, or the looming concern about others' perceptions. Toxic relationships or the loss of loved ones can also be triggers. Whatever the cause, anxiety is undeniably real and can be overpowering.

Navigating anxiety is an arduous journey, especially when it seems like nobody comprehends its weight. Yet, countless individuals share these experiences; we're not alone in this struggle. Its grip can infiltrate every facet of life, straining relationships and driving us to distance ourselves from those closest to us. It fosters self-doubt, undermines our confidence, and can manifest in physical symptoms like heart palpitations, sweaty palms, and breathlessness.

The key to combating anxiety lies in unraveling its roots, delving into what triggers these emotions. It's a daunting and often painful process, yet understanding becomes our first step toward reclaiming control. Learning to manage anxiety, finding healthy coping mechanisms, and seeking support when necessary mark our pathway forward. In this process, a glimmer of hope emerges, illuminating the path ahead.

Patience is vital; progress won't be instantaneous or effortless. However, as we confront anxiety head-on and learn to release control over what we cannot change, we gradually feel the weight begin to lift. Amid the chaos, peace becomes attainable, paving the way for stronger relationships, a renewed sense of self-assurance, and the rediscovery of life's beauty.

To those grappling with anxiety, remember that seeking help is acceptable; leaning on others and taking gradual steps forward are essential. Eventually, acknowledging that some burdens are too heavy to carry becomes necessary. So, release them; you cannot progress with the weight of a mountain on your shoulders. Letting go allows you to forge ahead unencumbered.

Relationship Cornerstones

Relationships are integral facets of our lives, sources of profound joy and fulfillment. Yet, amid the beauty they offer, it's crucial to recognize that every relationship, whether romantic, platonic, or familial, traverses its own peaks and valleys. These inevitable moments of strife and hardship are where patience and an open mind become indispensable allies.

Patience, often underestimated, holds a pivotal role in relationships. When adversity strikes, the instinct to seek immediate solutions can be overwhelming. However, healing and growth are gradual processes that demand time. Granting both ourselves and our partners the necessary space and time to navigate challenges paves the way for genuine resolution.

An open mind stands as another cornerstone of healthy relationships. Embracing each circumstance with a receptiveness to learn and understand diverse perspectives widens our own horizons and strengthens the bond we share with our loved ones. This openness fosters a creative and cooperative approach to facing challenges, enriching our relationships.

Accompanying an open mind, an open heart is equally essential. Engaging with others through kindness, empathy, and compassion creates an environment conducive to vulnerability and intimacy. These qualities deepen connections and nurture a profound sense of trust within relationships.

Effective communication acts as a linchpin, ensuring healthy interaction. Expressing ourselves honestly and transparently, while actively listening to the thoughts and feelings of others, fortifies understanding and trust in our relationships.

Respect, an invaluable facet, underpins healthy relationships. Upholding each other's boundaries, beliefs, and values cultivates an environment of mutual regard. Balancing the need for personal space with a willingness to collaborate and compromise bolsters the foundation of any relationship.

In summary, relationships thrive upon patience, an open mind, an open heart, effective communication, and respect. Cultivating these attributes fortifies the bonds we share, nurturing deeper connections and imbuing our lives with richer meaning and fulfillment.

Pure Heart

A pure heart is a remarkable thing, a vessel that feels deep, sometimes too much. It's both a blessing and a curse, especially considering the kind of people one encounters in life. It's not about naivety; rather, it's about being discerning. I'm vigilant with whom I allow into my inner circle, filtering most out. But when someone truly captivates me, I abandon my defenses and let emotions cascade freely. I surrender to the universe, embracing the emotions that engulf me without resistance. That's when the smallest gestures strike a chord within my heart, evoking immense joy.

Due to past experiences, I consciously choose not to let negativity cloud my happiness. Instead, I focus on the beautiful aspects, weaving elaborate fantasies filled with delightful moments. I daydream with eyes wide open, allowing myself to feel deeply for that special person. I'm driven to make them feel cherished, even if my expressions falter. Through subtle gestures, I ensure they know how deeply I care. There's an innocent purity within me that surfaces when the inner child takes the reins, guiding me to adore someone without reservation.

Yet, therein lies the challenge. When emotions run deep, so do the expectations. Despite my attempts to avoid it, subconscious desires breed expectations—expectations for reciprocity in care, priority, and love. The mind amplifies seemingly mundane gestures, interpreting them as declarations of affection. A smile feels like an affirmation of love, a touch like an intense longing reciprocated. It's a mental game, an internal narrative fueled by a heart that insists on proclaiming love. Gradually, even the rational mind begins to align with the heart's convictions. But reality intervenes abruptly, revealing the truth—I was foolish to attach so much significance to fleeting moments. What was monumental for me meant little to them. It's a heartbreak that eventually dawns upon me, unveiling the naivety and idealism within my heart. Yet, in hindsight, I acknowledge that perhaps my heart's purity was too extraordinary to find its match in this world.

Inclusion Essence

We often find ourselves confined within spaces that don't quite accommodate all that we are. It's a lesson ingrained in us—that there isn't a place capable of embracing the entirety of our being. So, we contort ourselves, attempting to fit into spaces that were never designed to be our forever home, merely a temporary abode. We're taught it's a fanciful dreamland, a realm of fantasy where our quirks and boldness don't belong.

The narrative we weave convinces us that our authenticity is too much, our voices too audacious for the norm. We internalize the belief that we're incompatible with anyone else's world, caging the essence of who we are. In a world where we're raised on a diet of inadequacy, it's no wonder we come to believe that we're not enough.

The venomous sensation of unworthiness claws at us when we entertain these thoughts. It feels toxic because it is. But the truth is starkly different. You are worthy. You are more than enough. Your voice deserves to reverberate. Your needs deserve acknowledgment, and your dreams deserve to soar.

Stand tall in your authenticity. Overflow with love, express yourself wildly, sing your song without inhibition, and chase your dreams fervently. Revel in the mystical elements that define you because with each unapologetic act, you strip away the layers of the disguise that society taught you to wear. Your naked truth shines through, attracting those who resonate with your authenticity.

Not fitting into the prescribed box isn't a failure; it signifies growth beyond constraints. It's a signal to break free, to transcend limitations and embrace the entirety of who you are.

Healing Path

I've discovered an ease in being the one left behind, lingering at the tail end of a line or strolling behind a bustling crowd. For years, I puzzled over why I didn't feel the urge to keep pace with everyone else, until a recent realization dawned upon me.

I cherish the unhurried journey through winding streets, navigating unfamiliar paths, occasionally losing my way, only to rediscover my bearings and stumble upon fresh perspectives. It's in these moments that I find solace, marveling at the intricate dance of the world around me.

I'm captivated by the subtle symphony of life— raindrops pattern against the ground, sunsets melt into sunrises, the moon unveils its shimmer, stars weave celestial tapestries, waves crash against the shore, wind whispers through trees, and birds serenade with their melodies. Each tiny fragment contributes to the canvas of beauty, unafraid to step away from the bustling crowds.

I'm not racing against time; I'm merely here, destined to arrive eventually. Embracing the journey has taught me to savor the process, to linger, and to breathe deeply. I'm learning the rhythm that best suits me, contemplating adjustments along the way, should they be necessary. I see myself as a work in progress, navigating through my own season.

All I seek is to wander, to explore, and to revel in the joy of living. Though I may walk a solitary path, I don't bear the weight of loneliness; rather, I carry a sentimentality that fills my solitary moments with depth and meaning.

Choosing Happiness

Life is an unpredictable rollercoaster, a captivating yet tiring journey. If there's one undeniable truth I've learned, it's the power of not knowing sometimes. Not knowing the whereabouts of those we've lost along the way or the destinations of the dreams we had to release—it's about embracing the beauty of the unknown, letting go of "what-ifs" and daydreams. I've spent too much time fixated on uncontrollable matters, missing out on cherishing the moments that truly matter.

Moments of pure joy slipped away unnoticed while I drowned in obligations and fixations on problem-solving. It's about time to shift the focus. I need more magic to fill my heart and peace to calm my soul. I'm choosing to abandon toxic influences, adverse situations, and negativity, opting instead for laughter, joy, and an adventure that makes me feel truly alive.

I've allowed the world's chaos to define my existence for too long. Maybe stealing moments for myself will reignite the spark I've been yearning for. It's about creating enduring memories—not of possessions or tasks completed, but of heartfelt laughter with friends, tender kisses in the morning rain, and feeling alive, loved, and connected to the universe.

Sure, life isn't perfect, and it can weigh me down, but I refuse to stay down. It's about standing tall, brushing off setbacks, and diving back into each day with renewed vigor. Some days may not go as planned, but I've learned that my happiness hinges on my choices.

So, I choose happiness in the moments that truly count. It's a journey—one that I know I'll navigate with resilience. I deserve happiness, and I'll seek it in the beauty of every moment that comes my way. One way or another, I'll find my way to contentment. That's a promise I've made to myself—one I always keep.

Energy Shield

Preserving our energy becomes paramount when we feel drained, isolated, or irate. It's during these moments that our outlook darkens, making it hard to appreciate life's blessings or feel gratitude. Protecting our energy isn't selfish—it's a vital act of self-care. The first step involves making decisions grounded in an internal locus of control. Refuse to succumb to external pressures; it's okay to reconsider plans or commitments made when you were in a better space. Take the liberty to not respond immediately to calls or messages or to choose solitude when needed. Embrace the liberty to rest, adjust your plans, or retire early without feeling the need to justify yourself to anyone.

There's a vulnerability that comes with fatigue and loneliness. Ignoring our body's signals puts us at risk of falling ill. Prioritize your well-being; it's okay not to offer explanations or apologies for seeking rest. You owe no one justification for your need to recharge. Protecting your energy and ensuring adequate rest are crucial for your overall health and peace of mind. Remember, taking care of yourself isn't a luxury but a necessity.

Tiny Triumphs

It's a common mantra to extol the virtues of hard work and perseverance, envisioning a future where we look back on our journey and celebrate our achievements. Yet, what about those of us who find ourselves stalled midway, despite dreaming big and pouring endless effort into our aspirations? We, too, should be able to look back and revel in our journey. I will. I'll cherish every small stride I took, remembering the moments I believed I could be anyone or anything and bravely pursue those dreams. I'll smile at the stumbles, knowing they were steps toward becoming a better version of myself.

The issue often arises when we only consider looking back once we've reached our ultimate goals, leading many to feel like failures if they fall short. But maybe we should reflect more often. Acknowledging how our small adventures and steps, even if they don't lead to our envisioned destinations, have impacted us and those around us can bring immense contentment and joy. This introspection holds more value than any accolade because it's about understanding the journey and its impact.

In the midst of your fatigue and the weight you carry within, it's okay to shield yourself and focus only on survival. Mistakes might feel like they erase past accomplishments, but they don't define your entire journey. Let people misunderstand you; their perceptions don't have to align with your truth. Living authentically, without conforming to others' standards, is the true goal. Trust in yourself and your reality as you tread the path of hope. Take a deep breath and believe that all your efforts, faith, and resilience will eventually bear fruit. It will all make sense someday.

Self-Worth

Understanding your worth is a transformative journey, a quest that ushers in positivity and self-cherishing into your life. Sometimes, believing in your intrinsic value can be an arduous path, but once recognized, it's akin to unearthing a hidden treasure within yourself.

Adopting the mantra "You are worthy" marks a pivotal step toward brighter horizons. It's a realization that you deserve kindness, love, and the abundance of good things life has to offer. This acknowledgment acts as a beacon, inviting positive energies into your world.

Self-love flourishes when you internalize your significance. It involves treating yourself with the same compassion and kindness you readily extend to cherished friends. It's about acknowledging your strengths and celebrating your achievements, regardless of their size.

As you firmly grasp your worth, it's akin to adorning yourself with a shield against negativity. You become more resilient, standing tall amid life's myriad challenges. Embracing your inherent value bestows upon you a brighter outlook, magnetizing positivity and nurturing an authentic sense of self-love.

The journey of recognizing your worth isn't merely a destination, it's a continual embrace, an ongoing affirmation that resonates deeply within, fostering resilience, self-appreciation, and an unwavering belief in your inherent significance. It's a symphony of acknowledging your essence and radiating that brilliance outward, attracting and celebrating the positivity that surrounds you.

About the Author

Ridhima Batra is a multifaceted individual, licensed social worker, entrepreneur, motivational speaker, and meditation practitioner. She's navigated significant challenges, having experienced clinical depression and anxiety from a young age, leading her to abandon engineering studies at 18. Amid this turmoil, her parents' counseling became a turning point, steering her toward mental health awareness and advocacy.

Harnessing her experiences, Ridhima began conducting sessions on mental health in schools while battling her own panic attacks and acute depression during her college years. Her commitment to mental health awareness transcended borders, leading her to represent India at global events and host the Global Peace Summit in New York.

Empathy became her driving force, culminating in the establishment of the Empathy Welfare Foundation. This foundation focuses on mental health awareness and gender equality issues. Ridhima's journey involved personal healing through writing, leading her to spread messages of love and kindness. Her endeavors include authoring a book aiming to guide those who have lost themselves in the complexities of life.

With over 8 years of experience, Ridhima's impact

spans 200+ seminars and 40+ events, collaborating with international organizations and advocating for UN Sustainable Development Goal 4 (Quality Education) and mental well-being. Her accolades include recognition as one of the Women Entrepreneurs of 2020 by Insight Success and receiving the Women Achiever Award from Khalsa College.

Despite her struggles, Ridhima has forged a path to empower and support individuals dealing with mental health issues, embodying resilience, and inspiring change through her empathetic approach and advocacy efforts.

www.ingramcontent.com/pod-product-compliance
Lightning Source LLC
Chambersburg PA
CBHW021401160726
47994CB00007B/3034